HUGH JENKINS

One of the unique distinctions of Annapolis, the one that may strike the traveler even before he arrives there, is that this city is the one state capital in the nation which cannot be reached by a steam railroad. But it was not ever thus. As a person of color once expressed it to an agitated man on the station platform whose watch proved to be slow, "Yas, suh, the train's done been and gone." In the Good Old Days, a vague epoch with which this book will deal extensively, there were two steam railroads. On one of them the startled passenger would have recognized no less a personage than Rudyard Kipling punching the tickets. At any rate, he was the identical image of Rudyard. Strangers, fascinated, would eye him during the entire journey from Baltimore, wondering if it really could be the author incognito, making an honest living on the railroad, and half expecting him to murmur that there's a Burma girl a-settin' or that they're hangin' Danny Deever in the mornin'. But despite the amazing resemblance — glasses, walrus mustache and all — you came to the reluctant conclusion that he must be someone else, for he spake neither in prose nor in verse. Only as the little train slid into the station at the end of the route he would open the door of the car and announce the name twice in a mild tone, the first with a rising inflection like a question, the second, as a reply: "Nap-liss? Nap-liss." He never varied this formula in thirty years.

From *Annapolis* by William Oliver Stevens, 1937

Henry Schaefer in his studio [1888-95]

An Annapolis Portrait, 1859-1910

"The Train's Done Been and Gone"

A Photographic Collection by MARION E. WARREN AND MARY ELIZABETH WARREN

Introduction and Text by MARY ELIZABETH WARREN

with Essays by

Published by
DAVID R. GODINE IN ASSOCIATION WITH M. E. WARREN
Boston, Massachusetts

[cover] *First bridge over Spa Creek* [1887-97]

[front endleaf] *Bird's-eye view by Sachse* [1858]

[back endleaf] *Dedication of the Southgate Fountain,
Church Circle* [May 1903]

Acknowledgments

We are indebted to many persons for inspiration and insight. To Mr. George Forbes, the self-appointed custodian of Annapolis' history, we are particularly grateful. His foresight in accumulating visual documentation in the early days of the Twentieth Century, and cataloging these drawings and photographs for future scholars, saved from neglect or permanent loss much of the substance of this volume.

Dr. Edward Papenfuse and the excellent staff at the Maryland Hall of Records, especially Phebe Jacobsen and Diane Frese. We greatly appreciate their cooperation and trust in making accessible to us a wealth of primary and secondary materials.

Historic Annapolis, Inc. for constant encouragement and interest for this project and their recognition and use of early photographs as a restoration tool.

The many who have searched their drawers and attics and made the photographic treasures they found there available to us, particularly Capt. Frank Munroe, Jr., USNR, Mr. Kent Mullikin, Misses Margaret and Virginia Worthington, Mr. and Mrs. Jack Francis, Miss Anna Douglas Valk, Fr. Patrick Lynch, C.S.S.R., Mr. Edward Lee, Mrs. Andrew Musterman, and Mr. William Cadell.

The publishers, Dodd, Mead & Company who graciously permitted us to quote from their book, *Annapolis* by William Oliver Stevens.

The Lapides Foundation and Mrs. Carleton Mitchell for their special interest and encouragement.

The *Preservation Press* of *The National Trust for Historic Preservation*, particularly Diane Maddex, for their supportive consideration of this project.

Calvert and Gordon Chapline for their extraordinary support and superb craftsmanship in printing, and Gerard Valerio for his excellent design assistance.

Most importantly, to our contributors, Mrs. J. M. P. Wright, Orin M. Bullock, Jr., FAIA, Arthur C. Townsend, and Lee Merrill, who gave not only their time and attention, but also their own creative talents, which greatly enrich our own efforts.

This project has been made possible in part by a grant from the Youthgrants in the Humanities Program of the *National Endowment for the Humanities*, a Federal agency established by the Congress of the United States of America to promote research, education and public activity in the humanities.

Names of Streets

you know

Names of public places

a - state house
b - college — all denominations
c - church St Anne protestant
d - court house too many lawyers
e - farmers bank (Md.) no pat no business
f - jail a few Irish

h - common or burying ground for old sooner or later
i - Hallam theatre wooden decaying for disuse
j - Catholic chapel St Cecilia — 2 times a month
k - Hughes' steam mill
l - Jones steam mill
m - market held every day
n - City hotel Swann & Iglehart pushing ahead
o - ball room old court house well attended
p - government house
q - fort Severn useless
r - garrison barracks Col Walbach
s - governors pond
t - fishing pond
u - swimming pond
v - Strawberry hill
w - powder house hill
x - college green
y - Ch. Carrolls old seat
z - Jones wharf

Private Localities

1 J. Hughes
2 Iglehart
3 Selby
4 Gambrills old tavern
5 McNeir
6 Old Nick Brewer
7 7 building So Domingo
8 Crabbs post office
9 Jonas Green
10 Wm Green
11 Mrs Gloves where Miss Fanny once lived
12 Wm Somerville Pinkney
13 Methodist meeting
14 Dr Ridgely
15 Col Sudler
16 Dr Sparks
17 Franklin Inn Mrs Bowie no patronage
18 City Hall
19 Dr Claude
20 G. Munroe
21 Mackubin
22 Dr Rany
23 Coulter
24 Mrs Jacob
25 Jack
26 T Johnson
27 Mrs Holland
28 Basil Stephens
29 P. A. Lively
30 G. White
31 Goodman
&c

32 Maj Jones'
33 Caulston
34 Geo Wells
35 Anna Harwood
36 Harry Harwood
37 Steele
38 Lockerman
39 Pinkney
40 Genl Harwood
41 J. Franklin
this street badly made

42 Brice
43 Randall
44 Randall
45 Eli Wells
47 Col Boyle
48 Vock Severn new house
49 Ramsay Waters
50 Dr Smith
51 Magruder Watkins &c
52 Mrs Murray
53 Primary School
54 Brice Brewer & grandd
55 Adam Miller
56 his store
57 Nicholson
58 Crabb

From Claude family correspondence

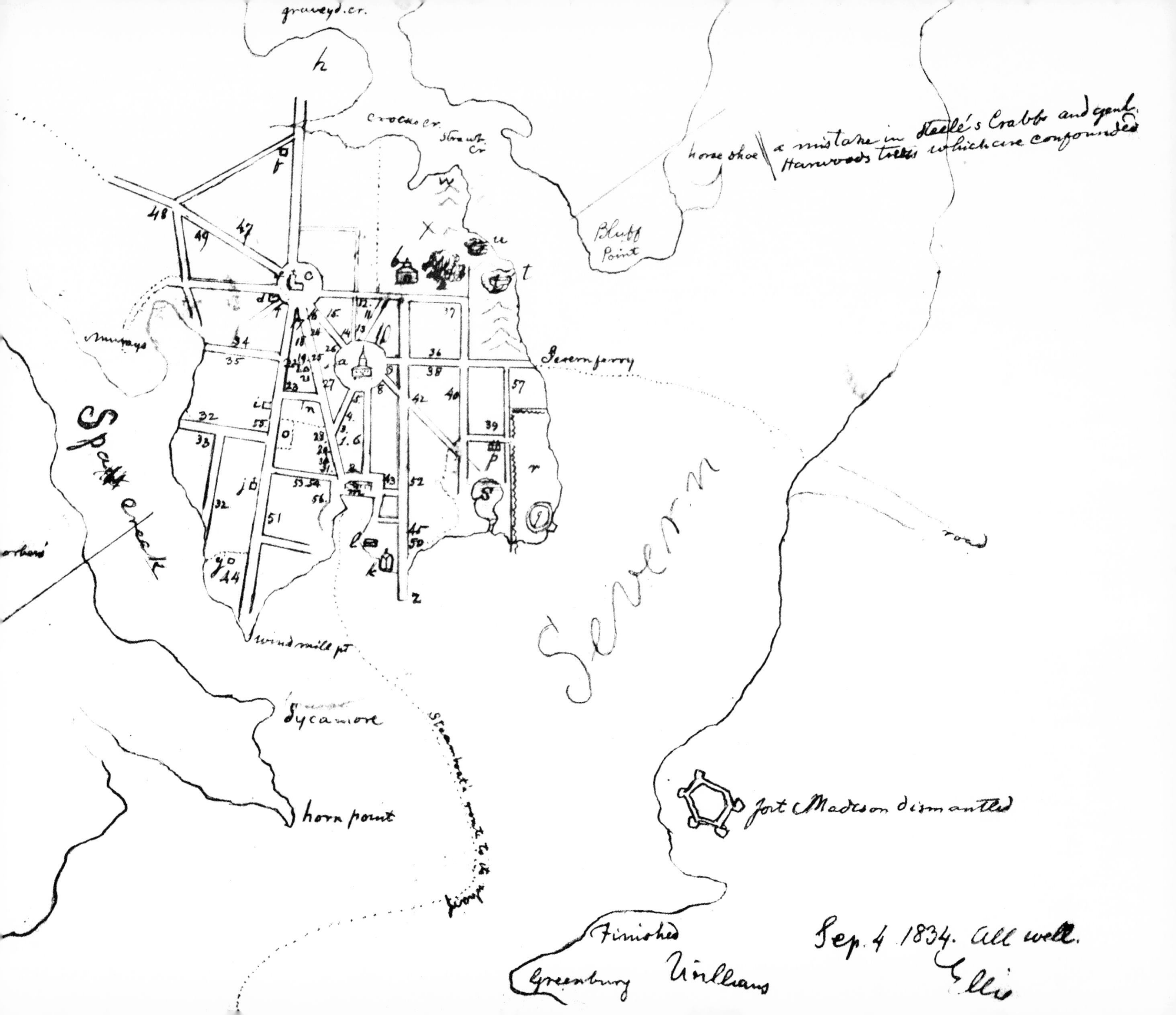

graveyd. cr.

h

Crocker cr.

Strawb Cr.

horse shoe ‖ a mistake in Steele's Crabb and gentl. Hanwoods tracks which are confounded

Bluff Point

48

49   47

f

c

d

murrays

Severn ferry

34

35

18 16 15

18 24 14 13

19 25

23

27

17

36

38

42   40

57

Spath creek

32

33

55

m

o   28

26

29

31

n

39

P

r

arthur's

32

j

53 54

56

51

q

44

l

43 52

45
50

k

z

Severn

road

S

q

wind mill pt.

Sycamore

horn point

Steamboat route to &c from

Fort Madison dismantled

Finished
Greenbury Williams

Sep. 4 1834. All well.

Ellis

Introduction

Imagination often romanticizes our sense of the past, whether the memories are our own or those gleaned from tradition or textbooks. For better or worse, photography enables us to remember with a more factual perspective the way life has been since the invention of the camera. We are now able to participate, at least visually, in life as it actually was over one hundred years ago.

This portrait of Annapolis between 1859 and 1910, the years of the earliest known photograph to the arrival of the automobile, is presented as a pictorial narrative, not only of a city, but also of an era. While the immediate subject *is* Annapolis, and the characteristics which make the city a unique urban district are stressed, an overwhelming sense of universality prevails.

Accumulating this collection has been both a challenge and a pleasure. Old and new friends have made contributions of photographs and facts, as well as suggestions for additional sources. This kind of personal involvement and the content of the photographs themselves have made this a people-oriented venture. While it is hoped that this volume will be of concern to scholars of the period, its primary intent is to acquaint today's reader with the Annapolitans who populate the pictures.

Dating the photographs posed a particularly difficult problem.

Early copies of the daily newspaper proved to be an invaluable tool, helping to establish when businesses were in a certain location, thus narrowing the time frame during which a photograph could have been taken. In addition, this research revealed a great source for contemporary text for the book. Wherever possible, articles from *The Evening Capital* are employed to explain or complement the illustrations; these newspaper items convey as no modern paraphrasing could, a sense of the town's self-image, in the vernacular of the period.

These photographs are for the most part the work of professional or gifted amateur photographers. The very earliest views are by C.H. Hopkins, a set of stereopticons illustrating an almost complete panorama from the State House dome (*left and following page*). Henry Schaefer, a German-born photographer who maintained a studio on Main Street from 1888 until his death in 1895, is pictured in the handsome self-portrait on page 2. Much of his excellent work appears throughout the book. Others whose works are represented here are Mr. Lynn McAboy, a Mr. Cassler, and E. H. Pickering. Unfortunately, many of the photographs are unsigned. We are grateful to these artists, and to those who valued their work and preserved it, that we may also experience the charming city which they captured on film.

Church Circle from the State House dome [1860-66]

Saint John's College

Bordley-Randall House

Maryland Avenue

Chronicles

1861
February, Annapolis is connected to Baltimore and Washington, D.C. by telegraph

United States Naval Academy relocates in Newport, Rhode Island for the duration of the Civil War; Academy grounds transformed into a hospital

Saint John's College suspends activities, is confiscated by federal troops for a parole camp, later moved two miles outside the city.

1864
Annapolis barbers determine to work on Sundays no more

1866
U.S.N.A. returns to Annapolis

1867
The town clock is situated in Saint Anne's Church

1868
The Mutual Building Association of Annapolis constructs the first bridge across Spa Creek

1872
December, a statue of Chief Justice Roger Taney unveiled in front of the Maryland State House

1879
June, Rescue Hose Company No. 1 organized

1882
Bay Ridge Resort opens

December, a local prohibition law goes into effect

1883
Independent Fire Company No. 2 established

1884
12 May *The Evening Capital* begins publication

1885
Annapolis Glassworks starts operations on Hor Point

March, one evening the town clock struck the hou and continued to chime, causing *The Evenir Capital* to comment: "It is not often . . . th

City Dock and Horn Point

City Hotel to Spa Creek

Charles Street and Acton Place

polis institutions or her citizens do more than allotted share of duty, and we regard this on the part of our town clock as really orious and worthy of record . . ."

rwitch Hook and Ladder Company organized , prohibition repealed, the city fathers ting that the law had been less than effective

rch, Shortline Railroad makes first run from n Street station

tizens of Horn Point resolve to call their village rn City"

vening Capital editorial suggests that the city rs consider "the connection of Compromise t with the Spa Bridge either in a direct or ed line"

1895
18 September, ten thousand excursionists parade through Annapolis at midnight, many businesses and homes being illuminated for the occasion; the *Evening Capital* reported, "many of the streets were flooded with humanity from curb to curb . . . there wasn't room to spit."

1896
May, the Board of Trustees of the Chase Home decide to charge twenty-five cents to visitors to the colonial landmark, and to require a fee of one dollar for artists or photographers taking pictures of the interior

1900
October, Annapolis Lodge No. 622 Benevolent Orders of Elks is instituted in the Shaw House

1901
1 January, new Post Office and Customs House opens on Church Circle

1902
18 May, Colonial Theatre opens in former City Hotel

1905
Annapolis Banking and Trust Company opens its doors

1906
"Anchors Aweigh" is composed by Lieutenant Charles A. Zimmerman, Bandmaster of the Naval Academy Band, while residing at 138 Conduit Street

1907
8 April, new bridge over Spa Creek opens to traffic

1908
March, W B & A Electric Line begins running streetcars on the streets of Annapolis

11

Interpreting the Historical Photograph

The time in which we are living might well be known as the age of photography. It is at least possible to believe that of all the wonderful discoveries or inventions of the nineteenth century that photography is the most important, and that it will prove more far-reaching in its effects than any other since the invention of printing. The invention of printing was the discovery of a method for the preservation and multiplication of the record of human thought; the invention of photography was the discovery of a method for obtaining the preservation and the multiplication of records of fact. Printing can only record what man knows or thinks; photography can record many things which man does not know and has not seen, much less understood. In photography, there is no personal equation. What a man has photographed is different from what he has seen or thinks he has seen, from what he declares he saw, from what he draws. Within limits it is an accurate statement of what was. Hence, photography is one of the most valuable of the tools of science, at once a means of research and an invaluable, because impersonal, record. Its applications are infinite, and we are probably only at the beginning of them. It has become the indisposable tool not only of the natural sciences, but of everything that touches upon science, of every study in which fact is of more importance than opinion or feeling. It will make history something different in the future from what it has been in the past . . . — Kenyon Cox in Scribner's Magazine, *May 1898*

Photographs present the historian with a visual record of a "moment in time" stopped indefinitely for his inspection. As such, it provides a direct record of how things and people looked, in a way that endless accounts of written records could never achieve. This "direct record" becomes then the invaluable tool of studying nearly all aspects of the visually recorded past, from architecture and its changing styles and lost examples, to costume design and grooming habits of those who lived in the age of the captured image.

The photograph contains an enormous quantity of internal factors, all of which can be studied and could be important to historical understanding. The camera often captures man doing what he does best — being a social creature, interacting with his fellow man. The result of photographs of this nature is a developed understanding of gestures and facial expressions which are available from no other source. Furthermore, from this visual record, the subtleties of social and individual ideas and attitudes may well become apparent and add considerable dimension to more broadly held social conventions widely written about.

Similarly, the interaction of people and things in the historical photograph can point to certain elements of economic and social condition. That which is photographed and who is photographed helps us to develop an understanding of the values at play within a given society. Photographs can, for instance, play an invaluable role in recording aspects of society which are avoided in written materials; the commonplace, the mundane and the illegal. Thus, often the historian's understanding of a given aspect of social nuance is from the photographer tredding where writers would not or could not.

Of course, using photographs in a systemic or scientific manner often means that the historian must be able to date his images. More often than not, photographs are undated and thus only datable from internal evidence. The "reader" must develop an index measure derived from content analysis of the group of photographs being used. In all cases, the researcher should choose items which have the greatest change rate — hairstyles, clothing and, when appropriate, automobiles — for indices. It is in this area that trade catalogues provide excellent source materials for this procedure.

While photographs speak to the trained scholar in numerous ways, probably the most interesting and least appreciated is the imprint of period material culture on the environmental fabric. When one thinks about mud streets receiving and retaining the mark of those who have passed over them, the pattern of wagon wheels, hobnailed boots, and bare feet, this begins to speak of levels and patterns not clearly understood, but fascinating to think about. Even the brick streets of Annapolis developed an imprint which hints of other aspects of the society. In photograph after photograph, horse manure abounds. This brings to mind the

Main Street at Francis Street [c. 1870's]

smell, systems for removal, and proper footwear or lack of it to deal with the problem. One small aspect can begin to build a network of relationships and questions, leading to understanding.

These patterns of material culture move beyond the streets and are evidenced in the photographs of any city from its roof tops. In summer, gardens abound and are in view, and by fall they are supplanted by huge stacks of split wood, again directing our thoughts to the systems within. Surely such patterns exist today. However, the photographs of the Nineteenth Century seem much richer in the very texture and fabric of a more basic and simplified existence.

One of the greatest qualities of the photograph in the long run is the way in which it presents a changing model of a culture over time. Take for instance the series of photographs of Annapolis' Main Street (then Church Street), ranging from sometime in the 1870's to approximately 1908. What is the most evident is the shop of James Hopkins; what one perceives is the rise of Hopkins' fortune and the store's changing facade. There is also the increasing network of electric lines and the introduction of street lights (technological changes), the appearance of post boxes (communication) and street cars (transportation), and on and on. All speak of the changing economics, values and attitudes of the society. The longer one looks, the more one sees. With the development of systematic scholarship in the use of photographs, new understanding will begin to emerge from the latent image.

The surfacing of new collections, the development of a system for "reading" a photograph, and a commitment to photographs, like the commitment to books, will bring this vastly under-utilized and under-rated resource into its own.

ARTHUR C. TOWNSEND *Director,*
The Watkins Community Museum
Lawrence, Kansas

[before 1890]

[1890-91]

[88-90]

[c. 1895]

[after 1908]   15

Duke of Gloucester Street

School Street [before 1893]

NAMES OF OUR STREETS

The curious and historic names of the streets in Annapolis are interesting to strangers, many of whom inquire into their origin. For the benefit of some of the residents who themselves do not know the associations, the following is appended:

King George Street was named for George II and Prince George Street for George III but of course these names were given before the Revolution. Conduit Street's origin is shrouded in darkness. It is supposed to have been simply a conduit or connection between Church Street and Duke of Gloucester Street as it formerly only connected these two thoroughfares.

Duke of Gloucester Street is said to have been named for the cousin of George III and this Duke of Gloucester, strange to say, was the first to inspire LaFayette to espouse the cause of the colonists. He himself is said to have admired their pluck and resistance of taxation and to have been the first to implant in LaFayette the burning desire to "come over and help in a just and righteous cause."

College Avenue is a modern name. It was Tabernacle Street. The square about the postoffice, Carroll and Northwest Streets was originally called Bloomsbury Square. No one seems to know how Shipwright Street got its name, unless at its end at the creek there was a shipping interest in those early days of the colonies. Randall Street was named for a former Mayor of Annapolis, John Randall, an ancestor of the family of that name now here.

It is pleasing to note that the original name of "Chancery Lane" has been restored to Franklin's Alley, thanks to the intercession of ex-counsellor W. Hallam Claude, when the new signs on the streets were recently placed.

Francis Street is named for Governor Francis Nicholson. These are only a few streets with interesting historical associations as to names that attract the attention of visitors, but are noticed daily by residents with the greatest unconcern.

The Evening Capital, 24 February 1904

Conduit Street [c. 1865]

18   *West Street [after 1880]*

Hanover Street from Maryland Avenue

Prince George Street from College Avenue

Cornhill and Fleet Streets

19

THE PRESENT ANNAPOLIS

THE VENICE OF THE CHESAPEAKE

Its Substantial Growth and Attractions —No Longer the "Ancient City."

We have so long been accustomed to hear of Annapolis as the "ancient city" a finished and sleepy town and a colonial fossil of decay and dilapidation, that after an absence of thirty years those who again rejoiced in the privileges of patriotism during the recent session of the Legislature were surprised to find that the old Annapolis had been supplemented to a large extent by a new and thrifty town to welcome the novelty of their reappearance at the State capital.

The new Annapolis, developed within the last twenty-five years, includes Eastport, West Annapolis, Germantown and other suburbs adjoining the original limits of the city of Queen Anne's time, and has a population certainly of ten thousand. Within this period the old town has been largely rebuilt by the addition of other stories or older houses replaced by new ones. Large areas have been covered with neat and often elegant modern homes and desirable locations within the limits proper of the city are becoming scarce. A marked tendency to become a place of retirement and residence for naval officers and others is shown in the many tasteful cottages and modern colonial houses recently erected.

Excepting Hagerstown, perhaps, no town in the State has grown more within the last two decades and assumed the garb of modern life in all the appliances in municipal need and civic comfort than Annapolis. The steam fire engine and its auxiliary hose and salvage corps, a uniformed police, electric light and gas, extensive waterworks, water which analysis shows to be second only in purity among the cities of the country, telegraph and telephones, railroad communications maintained by twelve trains daily, the paving of old and the opening of new streets, have been successive steps of progress.

The seat of government of Maryland since 1694, for half a century past Annapolis has been identified with the navy, and their wedded interests and associations have become an inseparable bond, cemented by the memories of youth, by marriage, and by the reunion of comrades seeking repose for age within the shadow of their alma mater. Fifty years (1845-1895) have been long enough to create a sentiment of attachment to the locality, and a proposition to remove West Point to Denver or one of our Western forts would be as great a shock to our soldiers as to ask our soldiers to abandon all the associations which the name of Annapolis recalls.

The new Annapolis has fifteen churches and chapels, three colleges, St. John's, the Naval School and St. Mary's Seminary. There are eleven schools, three being public schools. Five libraries are accessible to all and three bookstores indicate the literary demands of the place. The daily circulation of the *Sun* is large, and six newspapers are published in Annapolis, including one daily afternoon paper. There is an orphan asylum, and the Chase mansion has been given as an aged women's home, but awaits the requisite endowment. There are two banks, the Farmers' National and the Savings Banks.

As the county seat of Anne Arundel and a port of entry since 1695, the records of the county and the custom-house, stored in Annapolis, are of great historical value, although the lack of a suitable depository for the latter precludes their examination. A federal building for the postoffice, the custom-house, and a proper preservation of its records is a pressing need.

Arundel-on-the-Bay is an offshoot of Washington enterprise, and as an annex to Bay Ridge an objective point for the proposed direct road to Washington, the only remaining link in rapid transit to insure the rapid development of this beautiful region of Maryland.

Approached from the water the twelve spires and domes of the churches and public buildings of Annapolis give a picturesque impression, and with its eight bridges connecting the insular city with its suburbs suggests a Venice of the Chesapeake. It is to be hoped that with the return of the next Legislature the habitual presentation of the capital as a dilapidated relic of antiquity will cease, and Annapolis be spoken of as it is and not as it was under Queen Anne.

[*preceding pages*] *View from the State House dome, Main and Conduit Streets* [*about 1891*]

North Street to Main Street by Sachse [c. 1850]

Detail, Main and Francis Streets [1888-90]

Artists and photographers quickly recognized the extraordinary vantage point provided by the dome of the State House for recording panoramic views of Annapolis. From this elevated perspective the viewer at once enjoys an intimate glimpse into the city's backyards and an overall vista of the urban design and its environs.

Above, Sachse's comprehensive drawing reveals a sparsely developed Maryland Avenue, but dense population from East Street to Main (formerly Church) Street.

The view on the preceding pages illustrates several elements which give Annapolis its unique personality: gems of colonial architecture (the Ridout, Scott, Dulany and Carroll the Barrister houses) integrated with Victorian structures; its insular setting (Spa and Back Creeks define the land formations at top of photograph); and small industries (canning operations on Compromise Street and the glassworks on Horn Point) and retail establishments coexistent with private residences (detail, *right*).

23

School Street to Church Circle [c. 1892]

Detail, 211 Main Street [1889-95]

Saint John's College [1888-95]

Astonished At Town's Size.

A young colored man but 32 years old, who lives at Bristol, this county, heas never been to Annapolis until to-day. Shortly after his arrival in town he met Robert Moss, Esq., a leading attorney here, and exclaimed: "Gee whiz, Boss, I didn't know dis place was so big." The man spent half the day "sizing up" the town before doing his Christmas shopping. Think of living 32 years within a short distance of the great Annapolis and never seeing it until today.

22 December 1906

Government House and Bloomsbury Square [before 1893]

The "Georgianization" of Government House (built 1866) in the 1930's was soon followed by the destruction of almost every building in this view, to make way for pseudo-colonial state offices.

25

East Street, center, Cornhill Street, right [c. 1889-92]

(*preceding pages*) Extremely harsh winters often caused the oyster fleet to be frozen into Annapolis' harbor, bringing that industry, and commerce in general, to a standstill.

[*preceding pages*] Cornhill Street, center [winter 1876-7]

Cornhill Street, center, Francis Street, right [c. 1889-92]

(*above and left*) Greenbury Point *sans* radio towers and Horn Point as farmland offer sharp contrast to their Twentieth Century development.

Bulkheads and Bucks: Evolution of the City Dock

From its beginnings in the 1650s as "Todd's Harbour," Annapolis' "Dock" has been the evolving center of the city's commercial and social existence. Since Todd's shipwright activities commenced on the shore of the then broad and deep cove inside the sheltering mouth of the Severn River, the cumulative encroachment of bulkheads and fill have reduced its extent and reshaped its form, largely in broad response to the changing requirements and expectations of the commercial activities of each era. (*compare shorelines pages 27 and 29*).

Still a fair if tight harbour in the early Eighteenth Century, the publicly built wharf across the head of the dock (close to today's Market Space building line) berthed ocean-bound brigs and barks loading thousands of hogsheads of Maryland's prized "sot weed" for England's lucrative tobacco trade. With Baltimore's rise and Annapolis' decline as an ocean port after the American Revolution, few major ships still called at the Dock. Consequently, few voices questioned further filling along the shallower Dock Street shore or even the steep-to southern shore under the hillside above Compromise Street until, by the 1870's, the Dock was a mere "slip" of its former expanse. While no longer suited to handling larger vessels, the Dock was still adequate to the fleet of more modest sailing craft which supplied the array of usually flimsy warehouses, packing sheds, and mills constructed on this new and hardly firm ground.

The one hardy and notable exception among these indistinguished commercial structures was the quasi-public Market House built on filled land behind an early Nineteenth Century head of the Dock bulkhead. It has proven a venerable social and visual focal point for Annapolis' unique dockside plaza. Its broad overhangs sheltered the storage and exchange of goods shipped on canal boats, pungys, and coastal schooners as well as the hinterland's bounty unloaded from the horse-drawn wagons which had journeyed in West Street to the Market. No doubt the strategic location of the Market at the intersection of so many lines and modes of transportation, coupled with its cool shade, invited many lingering conversations over the "News of the Day." One topic of such informal socializing during the winter and spring of 1885 must have been the nearby fledging "City Circle" project (*see next page*).

The expanse of filled ground from the Market south to the foot of Main Street had previously been a cargo handling and stacking yard (*see page 27*). With the loss of major shipping once bustling at the Dock, it found itself an untended waste, usually rutted by wagons and muddied by the guttered streams coursing down Main, Fleet, and Green Streets. It soon became the focus of Annapolis' unofficial motto to "do something about the City Dock" (frequently the result of building cheaper wooden bulkheads rather than investing in more durable and expensive masonry quays). A collective of public spirited residents, with some assistance from the more concerned merchants, claimed this ground as a park *"for the people"* and proudly staked the claim with a great mound of soil, trees, grass, gas lamps, walkways and aesthetic bollards. Though the artesian well and horse trough proved a popular service which would evolve with the times, as a park, the short-lived "City Circle" was little used by the citizenry, probably owing to its sense of separateness from the real attractions to people: the Dock, the Market and the line of stores surrounding the entire scene. Despite the noble intentions and selfless labors necessary to this undertaking, this ambitious green spot soon earned the epithet "Dog Turd Park," so actually it should beget little surprise that, true to the Dock's history of commercial progress, the trees were cut down and the park gave way to a service station to water those horseless carriages which arrived some twenty or so years later.

The gas station, the fish market at the head of the Dock (*see next page*) and the sheds on down Dock Street are gone now to provide stacking yards again, though cars are the ships and people the cargo. The old openness of the Dock afforded by these clearings has reminded Annapolis of her nearly forgotten original resource — a good harbour on the Bay. Perhaps as alternative car parking is developed outside the Dock area and economic pressure from the burgeoning boating and water-oriented activities continues to mount, some credence may be given to ideas of enlarging the remaining basin to a harbour again worthy of its original appellation of "City Dock."

LEE MERRILL
Urban Designer, City of Annapolis

Detail, City Dock [c. 1889-90]

Market Space [1891-95]

Detail, west side of Market Space [1891-95]

LOCAL NEWS OF THE DAY

The "City Circle"

Instead of *three*-hundred cart loads of earth having been dumped in the "City Circle" by the Improvement Association as stated by us in a late issue, we understand that very near *nine* hundred loads have been deposited as a preparation for grading and tree planting as soon as the Spring opens. As several hundred loads more of good earth could be added with advantage the association will be glad to receive any contributions of that kind from public-spirited citizens. With the exception of some two hundred loads generously contributed by Mr. J.S.M. Basil the Society has paid for this work and happily been able to give some employment at a season of unusual dullness.

The extent of the circle expands as obstructions are removed. It is twenty-five feet larger in diameter than the rotunda of the capitol at Washington, over one hundred and twenty feet. Efforts are being made to procure a handsome fountain or statue to ornament the centre of the circle and it may be reasonably expected that by midsummer we shall have another green spot added to our city, probably the first improvement of this kind, *by the people and for the people*, in the two hundred years that Annapolis has been a city. Several citizens propose to plant each a tree and give their personal supervision to its protection and growth.

— *The Evening Capital*, 21 February 1885

Detail, West Side of Market Space [1888-95]

28 May 1884

Market Space [after 1900]

A New Butcher in Market.

Our Annapolis butchers are to be met by a competitor in their line of business on Saturday morning next in the form of a stranger who we learn has already leased a stall in our market. If he can teach our butchers the art of dispensing meats at a lower rate than at present, the lesson will be, at least beneficial to purchasers generally. If this new comer sells his meats at more reasonable rates than others in that line of business, he will be welcomed as a *bon ami.*

Prices of Fresh Meats.

Porter House Steak, per lb. 14c
Sirloin Steak, per lb. 12½c
Rib Roast, per lb. 12½c
Round Steak, per lb. 10c
Chuck Roast, per lb. 10c
Pork, per lb. . . . . 8c. and 9c
Home-made Sausage, per lb. 7½c
Home-made Pudding, per lb. 5c
Fresh Vegetable Soup, per qt. 3c

Every Monday and Friday from 11 a. m. to 1 p. m., every purchaser is entitled to 1 qt. of fresh Soup, free of charge.

Home-made Pies baked fresh every day.

Every out-of-town customer will be treated to a *Free Lunch.*

Goods delivered free of charge to all parts of the city.

26 February 1898

Middleton's Tavern, Market Space at Randall Street

Perhaps the most haunting element of these early photographs is their ambiguity: constant change, growth, "progress;" yet an unrelenting sense that the essence always remains the same. Parades of humanity, *et cetera*, whether organized or spontaneous, are the everyday fare of Main Street — anywhere.

Main Street [c. 1870]

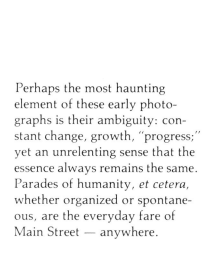

[preceding pages]
Main Street [1888-95]

38   *Main Street [c. 1890]*

Main Street above Francis Street [c. 1893]

118 Main Street [1888-95]

140 Main Street [c. 1893]

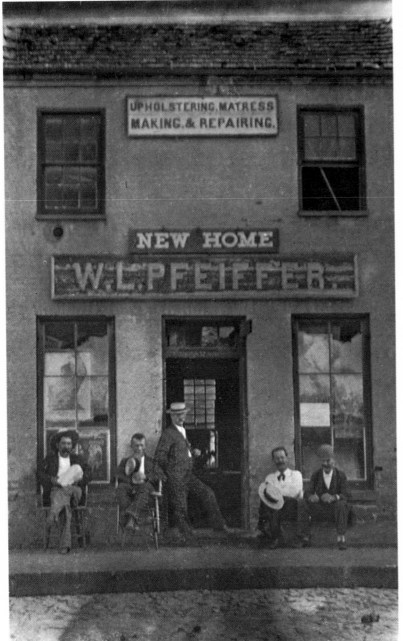

151 Main Street [c. 1893]

170 Main Street [after 1901]

1896

Daily publication of each day's guests at the Hotel Maryland made indiscretions under that roof all but impossible. Across the street were the less prestigious Kaiser House and (several doors down Main Street) Chesapeake House Hotels. While much of the south side of Main Street remained residential into the Twentieth Century, small retail establishments gradually prevailed. Business hours accommodated shoppers from 7 a.m. until 9 p.m. every day except Saturday — when most stores stayed open until midnight.

Maryland Hotel, Main and Duke of Gloucester Streets [c. 1890]

Main Street from Church Circle [c. 1890]

State Circle, Cornhill to Francis Streets [before 1902]

State House from
Francis Street [before 1901]

The establishment on State Circle second only to the State House in eminence was Wiegard's Confectionery. Its reputation for the finest sweets in town survives to this day in the memories of the former children who once delighted in its delicacies. Another venerable institution was Miss Annie Franklin's house (*left*), once the home of colonial cabinetmaker John Shaw. In 1900 it became the home of the Benevolent Order of Elks No. 622.

Shaw House [c. 1900]

47

Anne Arundel County Courthouse [before 1892]

The character of Church Circle changed dramatically with the arrival of the Twentieth Century. The impressive residences of the Forbes and Iglehart families gave way to the massive new post office and customs house, erected at a cost of sixty-four thousand dollars. The county court house had recently received a facelifting, adding a new entrance and cupola. In 1905 the Kaiser House Hotel was replaced by the Annapolis Banking and Trust Company, the first competition to Farmer's National Bank in ninety years.

Church Circle from College Avenue [after 1893]

Church Circle from School Street [before 1893]

[following pages] West Street from Church Circle [1892-3]

West Street [*c. 1910*]

These two photographs of West Street say a great deal about the state of the city in the years they were taken. *Left*, West Street was the approach *into* Annapolis, the capitol dome and Saint Anne's steeple looming as symbols of well-established urbanity at the end of a long and dirty road.

Above, the city's focus had begun to turn outward: the development of "suburban villages" — Murray Hill, Germantown, West Annapolis — was accompanied by all the modern amenities to help the traveler on his way.

53

Maryland Avenue from King George Street [c. 1870's]

Maryland Avenue enjoys the distinction of connecting two of Annapolis' most popular attractions: the Maryland State House and the United States Naval Academy. Along the route, however, are numerous landmarks notable for their own merit. At the corner of King George Street, the Hammond-Harwood House faces the Chase-Lloyd House, each an outstanding example of Georgian architecture. Elegant Victorian structures attest that the greatness of the city's architectural heritage extends beyond the Eighteenth Century. By 1900 Maryland Avenue was the address of commercial interests of every sort, and the Opera House at the corner of Prince George Street was the only large center of entertainment in town.

Maryland Avenue from Prince George Street [c. 1900]

[before 1881]

56 [c. 1904-5]

[before 1872]

Architectural Heritage: The Photographic Record

The buildings of Annapolis reflect the changing architectural taste of Marylanders down through the years. While many have gone the way of progress or neglect, good examples of Public, Private, Commercial, and Ecclesiastical buildings from every period remain. Some have retained the character imparted by their original designers, some have been "modernized", from time to time, while others have been subjected to a continuing metamorphosis and now find themselves restored to their original appearance.

The needs of changing owners have been met by the addition of amenities, or alterations to permit more contemporary uses, often accomplished with sympathy and appreciation of the quality of the original work. But, unlike the fate of many older cities in the United States, the humane character of this Colonial community has been retained.

The Capitol Building of Maryland, built in 1772-1780, is perhaps the most visible of the buildings of Annapolis because of its towering dome and belvedere or lantern. Though added to and considerably altered in plan through the years to accommodate the requirements of Government, the changes which have occurred on the principal facades are more cosmetic than architectural.

The site of the Capitol, State Circle, has been more radically changed through the years than any other part of the City. It is recorded that the proliferation of Government activities resulted in there being no fewer than eight buildings occupying the 538 foot circle, all of which were demolished when the present building, designed to replace them, was built.

Deeds, wills, and personal papers provide the restorationist with facts upon which the original appearance of a building may be conjectured; graphics made by contemporary artists may provide some visual evidence, but only since the days of photography has it been possible to accurately record the appearance of a structure at a specific period in time. Ghosted marks left in the painted surfaces when changes or additions have been made, worn places on floors, obvious more recent repairs, are welcome evidence of the former presence of a structural or architectural feature, but a photograph will positively confirm or provide more positive evidence of actual work which existed at a specific time.

Pictures of the Annapolis State House record the changing taste in the treatment of windows from the small panes in all of the windows before 1872, to large panes (two lights over two) in the first and second floors by 1881, and to the beginning of a restoration in 1904 when the windows of the Senate Chamber were re-fitted with small-paned glass. Today, all of the windows have been re-fitted with small paned sash.

The building was equipped with chimneys by 1881 and the picture seems to reveal the introduction of basement windows, which had not been provided during the first period of construction.

It appears that gas was used to light the State House until about 1904 when the gas lamp posts no longer appear in the pictures and wires may be seen crossing the corner.

An even more obvious transformation took place between 1881 and 1901 when a columnar porch was built to replace the pedimented frontispiece at the entrance. It is interesting to note that the new porch retained a vernacular use of the pediment reflecting the original doorway treatment, as well as the Ionic columnar order.

A close examination of the pictures of 1881 and 1901-04 reveals that ventilation was introduced into the drum of the dome by adding louvers in the bottom half of the windows. It would appear as well that the windows in the uppermost floor of the lantern were open until glazing was added by 1881.

By such comparisons of the photographic records of Annapolis buildings taken through the years, the changing history of its architecture may be found.

ORIN M. BULLOCK, JR. FAIA
Author of The Resoration Manual

[c. 1880]

Farmer's National Bank, founded in 1815, was for many years the only banking institution in Annapolis. This pictorial progression is evidence of its fiscal as well as physical growth.

[after 1892]

[after 1900]

Colonial Theatre [c. 1903]

[1895-1900]

The transformation of the City Hotel into the Colonial Theatre was a remarkable architectural adaptation. As the City Hotel, the building enjoyed a colorful history, including lodging George Washington the night before he resigned his commission as Commander-in-Chief of the Continental Army at the State House. In the Nineteenth Century it was a landmark of sorts: several businesses advertised their locations simply as "opposite City Hotel," or "next to City Hotel." By 1900 the establishment was in severe disrepair (*photo above*). As the Colonial Theatre, the building served as the setting for many and varied events, from the screening of some of the first "moving pictures" to enthusiastic audiences to the annual graduation of Annapolis High School students. The theatre and several surrounding buildings were totally destroyed in 1918 by a spectacular fire still remembered by many residents.

THE COLONIAL THEATRE

Tonight will mark an important epoch in the history of Annapolis, the seat of the first theatre in America. At 7:30 o'clock this evening the new and handsome Colonial Theatre will be dedicated. Mr. Elihu S. Riley, the Annapolis historian, will make the dedicatory speech, in which, in the name of the management, he will turn the new theatre over to the citizens of Annapolis.

Mayor Charles A. DuBois will accept it on the part of the city. Music will be furnished by the Naval Academy band. The doors will open at 7 o'clock, the exercises of dedication beginning at 7:30 o'clock and the performance of "The Holy City" will begin at 8 o'clock. The company arrived in this city last night, bringing their scenery and mechanical effects.

The new theatre has been built as an annex to the old City Hotel, where General Washington spent many nights. Indeed, the foyer has the same panels which the Father of his Country admired, and the same stairs leading to the balcony that were there in colonial times. But this is all that is colonial, the theatre in its plans and furnishings is strictly up-to-date in every particular.

There are six boxes on the ground floor, 190 chairs in the orchestra and 210 chairs in the orchestra circle, all antique mahogany veneered. In the balcony are 232 chairs of the same material. The gallery will comfortably seat five hundred persons, and is located above and back of the first balcony. The theatre has a proscenium opening, thirty feet wide and twenty feet high, back of which is a large stage, equipped with beautiful scenery from Lee Lash's studio, New York.

There are twelve dressing rooms. The curtain was painted by W. H. Labb, of Philadelphia, and is a work of art. The scene is taken from Holland, and includes a rustic stone bridge and sparkling streams. The fresco work of the walls and ceiling was designed and executed by Charles Hummel, of Baltimore, and when Electrician Boyd Dexter turned the current on the 360 electric lights Saturday evening the effect was magic and the view was most beautiful.

— *The Evening Capital* 18 May 1902

[1888

The Great Mansions

Because of the beauty, scale and setting of its early buildings, Annapolis was known in the Eighteenth Century as the Athens of America. Of those great mansions built between 1760 and 1774, seven are now National Historic Landmarks, recognized for their contribution to our national legacy. In many cities on the eastern seaboard, the rapid unplanned growth of the Nineteenth Century destroyed beautiful Georgian buildings and left others unrecognizable beneath new facades, cumbersome porches and ungainly additions. Annapolis largely has been spared these unfortunate changes.

The Ridout House (*see next page*) has remained in the same family since John Ridout built it for his bride in 1764. Maintained continuously as a private residence, the house has an imposing street Facade and a palladian window overlooks terraced gardens behind. Some modern improvements have been made, but basically the Ridout House has remained architecturally intact.

The nearby Upton Scott House on Shipwright Street served for many years as a convent for the School Sisters of Notre Dame. Despite certain additions made for their use, the interior was not unalterably changed and the exterior is intact. Today it is once again a private residence and ongoing restoration has shown the elegance of its interior woodwork.

The Peggy Stewart House (name for the brig belonging to the owner which was burned in protest to the imported tea she carried) was built c. 1763. Its traditional Georgian exterior was altered in 1894 when the roofline was changed from gable to hip, the chimneys were reconstructed to conform and a captain's walk was added. Early photographs indicate that the front porch may have been remodeled several times. The Anne Arundel County Board of Education owned the house in the early Twentieth Century, adapting the interior as administrative offices. The present owners have renovated the house as a private residence, duplicating as nearly as possible the original interior.

William Paca House, 1765, has endured several, also happily reversible, changes in the Nineteenth and Twentieth Centuries. Extra stories were added to hyphens and wings, and some of the interior woodwork was replaced. During the last century, this fine Maryland five-part plan mansion became a genteel boarding house and its garden grew vegetables for Navy families. In 1903 it became part of Carvel Hall Hotel, the main building totally obscuring the garden site. Archival and archaeological research, sophisticated analytical devices, use of sketches, photographs and, in the case of the garden, a detail in the Charles Willson Peale portrait of Governor Paca have guided the restoration of the house and garden by Historic Annapolis, Inc. for the State of Maryland.

The magnificent James Brice House, c. 1770, has had many owners, including Saint John's College. In the Depression years of the 1930's the College converted the interior of the mansion to apartments for its faculty. The present owners have faithfully restored the elegance of its interior.

The Chase-Lloyd House, begun by Samuel Chase, a signer of the Declaration of Independence, was purchased and completed by Edward Lloyd in 1772. It has a superb cantilevered stairway, palladian window and beautiful ornamental detail. The Episcopal Diocese of Maryland inherited the house under the will of Miss Hester Chase and now maintains it as a home for elderly ladies.

Hammond-Harwood House, 1774, William Buckland's masterpiece and the only house entirely attributed to him, is the most exquisitely detailed Annapolis mansion. After the death of the last of the Harwoods, it survived threats of removal to Henry Ford's Dearborn Museum Village and demolition for a service station. No vital changes have ever been made inside or out. The house is now owned and operated as a museum by the Hammond Harwood House Association.

With this rich architectural heritage Annapolis indeed deserves its modern title of "Living Landmark," both for the architecture itself and its environment, maintained with an integrity that is rare among cities.

Mrs. J.M.P. Wright
President, Historic Annapolis, Inc.

Paca House, 186 Prince George Street [after 1902]

Chase-Lloyd House, 22 Maryland Avenue

Paca House Garden [1860's]

Hammond-Harwood House, 19 Maryland Avenue

ANOTHER HOTEL

The Paca Mnasion Sold To William A Larned, of New York—Will Keep Colonial Architecture In Tact

The sale of the Paca Mansion on Prince George street, the old colonial residence which Winston Churchill, in his story of "Richard Carvel," locates as the home of Dorothy Manners, the heroine of the book, has been ratified and confirmed, and the deed was recorded on the last day of the year, December 31st, 1901.

The property was purchased by Mr. William A. Larned, of New York city, from the estate of the family of Richard Swann, of which estate Mr. John Wirt Randall is trustee. The price paid was $15,000, and Mr. Larned intends to make some changes in the place and conduct a hostlery there. The purchaser is a New England man, whose father is thoroughly familiar with hotel management, being the proprietor of several successful hotels in the Adirondack Mountains. It is understood the manager of one of these will take charge of the Annapolis hotel for Mr. Larned, in winter.

The proposed changes will consist of a large colonial porch, which will extend along the front of the mansion. A driveway will be constructed from the street, passing under the porch. A large dining room will be built in the rear with the kitchen connecting with it and the right wing. There will be an entrance also from the rear on King George street, and one on the side from the new street, which will be cut through from Maryland avenue, to be known as Harwood street. After the completion of the new Naval Academy, the new hotel will border on the limits of the Academy grounds.

The Paca House stands on the Northeast side of Prince George street, near East street, and was built by Governor Paca, who was Governor of Maryland in 1782. Arthur Schaal purchased the house from the Governor, and subsequently sold it to Louis Neth. Chancellor Theodore Bland lived there in 1847. In the rear of the house is a garden which was famous in its day, and which contains a spring, over which a fountain will be placed when the improvents are made.

3 January 1902

Ridout House, 120 Duke of Gloucester Street

Peggy Stewart House, 207 Hanover Street

65

Spa Creek [1864]

Mortuary Chapel

Saint Mary's Church from Spa Creek

The community at Saint Mary's Roman Catholic Church occupies some of the most valuable real estate in the city. Originally owned by Charles Carroll of Carrollton, a signer of the Declaration of Independence, the property once extended all the way to Compromise Street (*right*), making a direct route from Market Space to the Spa Bridge impossible. Over the years numerous uses have been made of the land, apparently including an enormous tomato patch, whose full extent is better seen in the view from the State House dome on pages 20 and 21.

Saint Mary's Church and tomato patch [c. 1891]

First bridge over Spa Creek from Saint Mary's Rectory, toward Horn Point [after 1885]

The Spa Bridge.

We have been requested by parties residing on Horn Point, and who have to travel daily over the bridge across Spa creek, to call the attention of the county authorities to its present unsafe condition. It is very much out of order, and the fear is expressed that unless immediate attention is given to the same, some accident may be caused therefrom at any moment, if in fact the bridge itself don't fall to pieces.

13 September 1884

A VERY DANGEROUS PRACTICE.

Sitting On Rail of Spa Bridge May Result Seriously.

The bridge over Spa creek that connects Annapolis with Eastport, that thrifty suburban village, is a popular rendezvous for young and old in the evening. The cool breezes that play over the creek are refreshing after a hot summer's day and all classes of people seek the bridge and stand or sit there on the rail for hours watching the small row boats or sailing craft on the creek and river, and taking in the beautiful prospect of the Naval Academy.

It is a pleasant source of recreation and is very popular but persons must be warned that the bridge is not safe. The Capital has emphasized this fact from time to time, and that some serious accident has not happened to those who invite risk by sitting on the rail of the bridge is due more to good luck than to good management. A party of young men and boys have a habit of sitting on the bridge rail directly under the electric light, night after night. The result is the rail broke down last night and fifty feet of it near the boathouse fell to the bridge. That no one was hurt or thrown into the water is marvelous.

The rail of the bridge is from 6 to 12 inches out of plum. It is unsafe and extremely dangerous to sit on it, and this ladies and men persist in doing nightly. The warning has been repeatedly given, and had better be heeded before it is too late, or some one may lose his life on a dark night by being precipitated into the creek from the habit of sitting on a bridge that is unsafe for such purposes and should be condemned, or rebuilt.

————

12 July 1905

Spa Bridge at Duke of Gloucester

Panorama of Annapolis from Horn Point [1901-2]

Compromise Street from Duke of Gloucester

In December, 1906, the City of Annapolis paid one thousand dollars to the Redemptorist Fathers for damages "for the purpose of connecting the present terminus of Compromise Street with the new bridge over Spa Creek to Eastport, where it enters the city at Duke of Gloucester Street. In addition, the City relinquished all claim to the contiguous water rights . . . "

Around The Wharves

The harbor is completely frozen over again, and there is no track in the ice today. At 11 a. m. no boats had been in or out of the harbor. The police steamer Governor Thomas, Captain Turner, is tied up to the wharf. Yesterday the Governor Thomas made a trip out to Sandy and Thomas' Points, with Captain C. E. Martin, of the May Brown, aboard. Captain Martin found the bay frozen from Sandy Point to Thomas' Point. There was a little free water, a narrow stream, between the ice near Sandy Point but there was ice from Thomas', to above Sandy Point. The present conditions of the ice are considered serious for the shipping.

18 February 1904

Beautiful Snow.

The snow storm which set in here on Thursday afternoon continued all through the night and part of the day yesterday and last night—covering the ground to a depth of from eight to ten inches on the level, with drifts from two to three feet. It is the heaviest snowstorm since the blizzard of 1899. The sun, however, rose this morning in all its glory and the day has been an ideal one for sleighing, and there has been a perfect carnival of sleighs of all classes. The day was a perfect one overhead and everybody has taken advantage of the beautiful sunshine. Owing to the depth and the heavy drifts in the roads, very few country people ventured to town during the early morning.

30 January 1904

Compromise Street, "the Great Freeze" [1893]

Everybody on Skates.

Everybody had a skate on this morning, not in the figurative sense, but in the literal. Ladies did their shopping on skates, men went to their places of business on skates., and children had a glorious and hilarious old time skating before and after school on the streets and sidewalks.

It was a gay and festive scene out of doors and a regular St. Paul and Minneapolis carnitval, but this time held in Annapolis. One lady was seen to skate up to the Farmers National Bank, walk in on her skates and attend to her financial affairs as naturally as if skating on the streets was an every-day occurrence.

Men For Horses

A countryman came to town this morning with a large market wagon loaded with produce. He did not think the vitrified paved streets of Annapolis were a delusion and a snare when covered with ice and sleet. By dint of good luck he reached Main street without a misnap, when the horse fell and was injured. It was useless to attempt to go further and the market was his destination. The horse was unharnessed and taken out of the wagon, which was pulled the rest of the way to the market by six men, who took the place of horses.

19 February 1904

Saint Anne's Church from College Avenue

Maryland Avenue from Hanover Street

Annapolis and Elkridge Railroad Station, West Street [c. 1870's]

The train *really* done been in Annapolis, as early as 1840; on Christmas Day of that year a passenger train made its first run. The Annapolis and Elkridge Station was located on West Street, interestingly, on the site of the present bus station. The twenty year span here illustrated reveals much tree growth; human activities remain remarkably unaltered.

[c. 1890'

Shortline Railroad Station, Bladen Street [1888-95]

A second railroad, the Shortline, began operations in March, 1887.
Hotel Wolfe's featuring both a European and American plan, opened the
same year, directly across from the Bladen Street station.

15 November 1906

Bladen Street Station
from State House dome [1888-95]

24 November 1906

STREET CARS RUN TOMORRO

A GREAT ENTERPRISE COMPLET

What Electric Road Will Do For Annap
—Town Must Improve—A Favorite
Residential City—What Others
Say Of It

Everything is in readiness for ru
ning the street cars of the W., B.
A. Electric line at regular interva
tomorrow over the streets of Annapo
Several cars were run over the rou
last evening and the dynamo at t
sub-station on West street seems to
running smoothly.

There was some hitch at the pow
house last Saturday, and the offic
party from Baltimore, consisting
Mayor, ex-Mayor and others that too
the trip from the state metropolis
the national capital thence to t
state capital were not able to go ov
the street route owing to a tie up
the sub-station.

This has all been remedied and th'm
are now running smoothly. It is
matter of conjecture to 75 per cent.
the Annapolitans whether or not t
electric line to Annapolis will bene
the town. There are any number
doubting Thomases. They must s
the number of tickets sold and mu
thrust their fingers into the mon
bags of the corporation from Clevela
that built the road and back, it befo
they believe it will amount to an
thing worth while.

"That part of the Washington, Ba
timore and Annapolis road whie
lies between the city limits of Balt
more and the District of Columb
passes through an undeveloped an
unimproved section of Anne Arund
and Prince George's counties. Station
have been established at interva
of three-quarters of a mile. T
country, while unimproved, is we
wooded and healthy, and with a so
well adapted to the production
vegetables and fruit.

"The road will probably have t
effect of bringing population to t
territory and promoting the growth
villages and the building of count
homes. Altogether, the opening
the Washington, Baltimore and Anna
olis road is an auspicious and high
important event.

Maryland Day, 1908, saw the official opening of the W.B. & A. Electric Line. The intra-city route began at the depot on West Street between Washington and Calvert Streets; from there it ran one block of West Street, around Church Circle to College Avenue, turning right on King George Street to Randall Street, into Market Space, up Main Street, around the other side of Church Circle and back out West Street to the depot.

Main Street, looking West from Market Place, Annapolis, Md.

Hotel Maryland, looking down Main Street.   ANNAPOLIS, Md.

Depot of Washington, Baltimore & Annapolis Electric Railway Co.   ANNAPOLIS, Md.

USING NEW DEPOT

W. B. & A. Has Adandoned Old West St. Station

The Washington, Baltimore and Annapolis Electric Railway Company has abandoned the old West street station used by their steam road, and recently used as the terminus of the new electric road.

Yesterday the Electric Railway Company's officials opened its headquarters at the new station, corner West and Washington streets, and is now occupying same. The new station is practically the terminal of the electric line, and persons not boarding an electric car in town will be obliged to go to this new terminal to take an electric car for Baltimore or Washington.

The large dynamos for the city is located at the new station.

7 April 1908

Fast Bicycle Riding.

As Spring opens and bicycle riding is more and more indulged in on the public streets, complaint is being made of the fast riding. Yesterday a gentleman was knocked down on College avenue, and the day before a child was run into on Prince George street. Some riders have little care for the safety of pedestrians and careless riding sometimes causes serious trouble If a few arrests are made for fast bicycle riding it will soon be stopped. Most of the bicycles have no bells, no lights after dark and are a menace to life and limb. Where is the bicycle ornidance and its enforcement?

14 April 1896

CYCLE CRAZE.

Annapolitans Have the Fever An Important Part of College Athletics.

Annapolis has the bicycle fever. Never before has so large a number of wheels been on our streets and roads. Where a single rider was seen a few months ago spinning along quietly on the road, now it is an uncommon thing to see parties of ten or twelve.

The fact of so many wheels being ridden, and the pleasure in a ride many miles out in the country, has attracted the attention of the business men, whose duties are so confining in a store, that the fresh air is appreciated by the assistance of the wheel. Then also those employed in the Naval Academy, who live at Eastport and Germantown, have found a big advantage in owning a bicycle.

Bicycle championship races will be a feature this year of the intercollegiate athletic contests. and in view of that fact experts in college athletics are laying about in an effort to pick the winners.

12 March 1904

West Street from Cathedral Street [after 1908]

West Street

Conduit Street at Main Street [c. 1890]

FEAR OF "THEM THINGS."

A certain undefinable, mystical fear fills the mind and heart of the residents of the county when an automobile comes choo-chooing in the locality of the farms in Anne Arundel. Women picking tomatoes in the patch will grab up their baskets and run for dear life when they see an automobile in their immediate vicinity. Other women, girls and children who are out in the garden will grab the younger children when an automobile whizzes by, run with them into the house and slam the door, as though they fear a real infernal machine is after them and intends to come into the solitude of their home.

There are still others that frighten at the sight of "one of them things," and the old colored mamies fall on their knees in prayer or call the children to "git out of de way, yer cums one dem things from town." Their fear is almost equal to the consternation wrought by the first steamboat that steamed up the Mississippi. Many of the horses are getting accustomed to the automobile, but many others are still fearful and rear and prance at the sight of a machine. Men driving alone endeavor to make the animal unsed to the sight of an automobile, but it is more difficult when teams with women and children are encountered.

Some have to get out, lead the horse aside and hold the bridle until the machine is well out of sight and hearing. It is a queer thing that bicyclists cannot ride behind an automobile. For some reason the cyclist wabbles from one side of the road to the other and seems to imagine there isn't room for him and the machine both to pass in the same road. Invariably the cyclist dismounts his machine and walks until the auto passes by. A few Anne Arundel horses are of the variety that will not frighten at anything, not even an automobile, and continue along in the even tenor of their jog trot way. Sooner or later the horse must get accustomed to the automobile and its noise and commotion on the public roads.

14 August 1905

Main Street below Francis Street [c. 1911]

Ultimately, the triumphant mode of transportation, here as else-
where, was the automobile. By tradition, the Valk family owned the
first car in Annapolis. *Above*, the Hamilton Gale, Sr. family poses
proudly in the latest model.

A NARROW ESCAPE.

Auto Turns a Street Corner Without The Honk Honk.

Mrs. L. L. Jeffers, the mother of Mrs. Anne Burton Jeffers, State Librarian, made a narrow escape from injury and possibly from death this morning.

Mrs. Jeffers was crossing King George street not far from Maryland avenue, when an automobile whisked around the corner of Maryland avenue and nearly knocked Mrs. Jeffers down. The automobile did not sound the horn or make any sign of its coming and no warning of its approach as it turned the corner made its coming, more dangerous.

Had the auto been going at the usual high rate of speed some of them still maintain through the city streets, the estimable lady would have been knocked down and probably killed. There are several very dangerous corners in town for teams and autos to turn without warning, and the law should be strictly enforced before there is a serious accident.

13 April 1907

3 November 1906

Annapolis' first fire engine imported from England in 1755

The names of Annapolis' fire companies, Waterwitch Hook and Ladder, Independent Hose No. 1, were more than just titular. Literally, the Waterwitch firemen brought the hooks and ladders to a fire, the hose company supplied the hoses and the engine company provided the power. As seen by the various emblems on their hats, the group *at right* represents several different companies.

Waterwitch Fire House, East Street

Municipal Building, Duke of Gloucester Street

East Street [*possibly 8 June 1903*]

Annapolis has been host and home to many celebrities through the years. The shoeless gentlemen *above* impressed an early photographer enough to be made the subject of one of the earliest photographic portraits taken in the city. Frank B. Mayer, pictured with Miss Annie Franklin on the porch of her home, was a noted artist and president of the Local Improvement Association.

88

Government House [1907]

MARK TWAIN HERE.

THE KING OF HUMORISTS THE GOVERNOR'S GUEST.

Brings Sunshine And Springtime Along With Him — Received With Quiet Dignity But Sincere Pleasure.

TO-NIGHT'S ENTERTAINMENT AT STATE HOUSE.

Mr. Samuel L. Clemens, better known as Mark Twain, the king of humorists, arrived in Annapolis yesterday afternoon at 4.20 o'clock. As if a sunbeam himself the sun greeted him upon his arrival and the pall that had hung over the sky for several days was lifted. The sun shone out brightly and the balmy air of springtime welcomed the distinguished author and humorist.

Mr. Clemens' visit here has been anticipated with pleasure for some days, but there was no gaping, curious crowd to meet him upon his arrival yesterday afternoon. There was no newsboys or bootblack mob, no ragged urchin element at the station, but all was quiet and reposeful and he must have been impressed with the placid dignity with which Annapolis received him.

Mr. Clemens was met in Baltimore by Governor Warfield and Col. E. L. Woodside, of the Governor's staff, who accompanied the world's funny man to Annapolis. With Mr. Clemens was Miss Lyon, of New York, a friend of the Clemens family. The humorist entertained the Governor and those in the immediate vicinity on the train en route to this city by telling funny stories to the enjoyment of all about him.

10 May 1907

21 State Circle

Ridout House porch

Main Street [1888-95]

THE SUNDAY EXCURSION

Fearfully And Wonderfully Made—
A Large Crowd,

A number of Annapolitans took in the Sunday excursion down the river yesterday. There was a pretty good crowd aboard, and an excursion like this is a good place to study human nature. The women were well dressed and the men made a good appearance, but not so much can be said for samples of education displayed in conversation that floated on the breeze.

Indeed it is surprising that there is such gross ignorance and such murdering of the English language when the public schools offer so much free. To hear people say "I would have went" and "seen" for "saw," is without excuse or reason these days of public schools, and is a reflection on the material the public schools turn out.

On yesterday's excursion one woman was asked when Mrs. —— left a river resort. Her reply was "Her left last Wednesday. I would have went then, but my week wasn't up." "I seen her, and she seen me" were frequently heard and from women arrayed in spotless white with their fingers loaded with diamonds. Everybody took along plenty to eat and some did nothing but eat from the time they started until they reached home. The average Sunday excursion is fearfully and wonderfully made.

14 August 1905

Spa Creek

Midshipmen and friend, Naval Academy

BLUE SUNDAY IN ANNAPOLIS.

Drug Stores in Mourning—No Cigars and No Soda Sold.

Yesterday was blue Sunday here. You could not get a cigar for love or money, no matter how bad you wanted a smoke, and as for a refreshing glass of soda, if you were so dry you couldn't spit, you had to grin and bear it. The drug stores were draped in mourning, and black cloth covered the show cases and soda fountains to indicate that the grand jury had passed the death sentence upon Sunday sales. A sickening gloom hung over the premises, and the man who had neglected to provide himself with cigars for the day, was not in a humor to be asked a favor. It was a blue Sunday from start to finish, even the skies were overcast throughout the day in which the Sunday law was rigorously observed.

4 May 1896

Francis Street at Main Street [c. 1893]

IT IS COMING!
LET ALL REJOICE!

FRANK A. ROBBINS'
DOUBLE CIRCUS, MUSEUM, MENAGERIE
—and—
TRAINED ANIMAL PARADOX
WILL EXHIBIT AT
Annapolis, TUESDAY, October 18th.

CHAS. W. FISH
CHAMPION OF THE
WORLD

WHAT YOU WILL SEE IN THIS
GREAT, NEW AND NOVEL SHOW!
TWO CIRCUS COMPANIES IN TWO RINGS!
DOUBLE ELEVATED STAGE PERFORMANCE!
MUSEUM OF HUMAN WONDERS!
MONSTER MENAGERIE OF RARE ANIMALS!

CHARLES W. FISH | **CHEV. IRA PAINE**
The one King Horseman of the Universe. | The Master Shot of the World.
A HERD OF MONSTER
EDUCATED ELEPHANT'S!
INCLUDING THE
$125,000 ELEPHANT BAND
Performing on a variety of Musical Instruments.
LINDA JEAL | **ELENA JEAL**
The only Lady Bounding Jockey Rider. | Champion Lady Bareback Rider.
WILLIAM } **The DAVENES** { LUCY.
Wonderful Aerial Artists and Champion Gymnasts.
MLLE. ALNA DANAJANATA,
The Oriental Snake Charmer, wrapped in Coils of Monster Reptiles.
THE ONLY CLOWN ELEPHANT
"ABDELENA."
TEN FUNNY CLOWNS!
AND
A HUNDRED STAR PERFORMERS
From Every Branch of the Arenic Profession, forming
One of the Grandest and Greatest Exhibitions on Earth!

A FREE STREET PAGEANT
Of Gorgeous Magnificence will be given at 10 o'clock, A. M., every day, starting from the place of
exhibition and proceeding through the principal streets. In this splendid Processional Display will
be seen a long line of Gilded Chariots, unique Vehicles of novel design, open Cages of Wild Beasts,
a herd of **Thirteen Elephants**, Ponies, Camels, Jubilee Singers, and THREE BANDS OF MUSIC.
DO NOT FAIL TO SEE IT. It will cost you nothing.

TWO PERFORMANCES DAILY. Doors Open at 1 & 6 P.M.
Which gives a full hour for seeing the many interesting wonders in the Museum and Menagerie,
before the Circus Performances begin.

EXCURSIONS on all Railroads at a Reduced Fair for Round Trip.
Full particulars can be had from your Railroad Agent.

1887

Main Street [c. 1893

Naval Academy candidates, 112-114 Main Street [after 1895]

THE GLORIOUS FOURTH OF JULY.

How The Day Was Spent By The Residents of This City And Vicinity.

What would be called a "sane" celebration of the Fourth of July was that of yesterday in Annapolis. Although the small boy was in force with his torpedoes, his fire crackers and other instruments of noise, the day was, for the most part, spent rather in quiet recreation than otherwise.

Practically every private residence in the city was draped in bunting and flags as was all the shipping in the harbor. At the Naval Academy the ships in port were dressed, a national salute was fired and all the men possible were given a holiday. The midshipmen engaged in ball games and other pastimes and there was no academic work of any sort. All of the engine houses in the city were draped in bunting and flags, the dome on the State House carried a handsome of flat and the postoffice and courthouse gave evidence of the day. Practically air business was suspended and for the first time in years all of the stores were closed.

A bread famine struck the town and those who had not had the foresight to lay in their provisions the day before went breadless. Not a loaf of bread was to be had in any of the stores and other supplies were equally hard to secure. The streets were fairly deserted during the best part of the day and evening there being fewer persons moving about than on Sunday. Picnic parties, large and small, left the city early in the morning and made for the various points a short distance from the city. Severn river, Spa creek, Hawkins' point, Weems' bluff and various other places received their quota of picnicers.

Practically every pleasure craft in the harbor was called into service and carried away a large crowd of excursionists. The picnic at Bouchers', at Galesville and other points took a large number of person from Annapolis and it was not till this morning that Annapolis received back all of its residents. As far as is known there were no serious accidents to mar the day.

5 July 1904

41 West Str

MARION E. WARREN settled in Annapolis thirty years ago; as a professional photographer he has documented visually his environment in the present and collected and preserved its images from the past. He has received numerous national and regional awards for his photographic abilities and contributions to his profession. "Historic Annapolis," a one-man show circulated by the Smithsonian Institution for three years to museums, colleges and universities throughout the United States and "New Life for Landmarks" which opened in New York and toured the country extensively are among his many exhibitions. With his wife, Mary, he published *Annapolis Adventure*, a photographic essay of Maryland's historic capital.

His daughter, MARY ELIZABETH, is a native Annapolitan. She holds a degree in English Literature reflecting a continuing interest in Victorian England. It was with great delight that she discovered the charm of her birthplace during that same era.

Composed in Palatino by Fishergate
Publishing Co., Inc., Annapolis, Maryland.

Printed on Warren's Lustro Offset Enamel
by Wolk Press, Inc., Baltimore, Maryland.

Designed by Gerard A. Valerio